Snow White
and the Seven Dorks

A Readers' Theater
Script and Guide

By Nancy K. Wallace • Illustrated by Nina Mata

visit us at www.abdopublishing.com

To my daughters, Mollie and Elizabeth, who have spent endless hours helping with library plays! —NKW

Printed in the United States of America, North Mankato, Minnesota.
042013
112013
♻ This book contains at least 10% recycled materials.

Written by Nancy K. Wallace
Illustrations by Nina Mata
Edited by Stephanie Hedlund and Rochelle Baltzer
Cover and interior design by Renée LaViolette

Library of Congress Cataloging-in-Publication Data

Wallace, Nancy K.
  Snow White and the seven dorks : a readers' theater script and guide / written by Nancy K. Wallace ; Illustrated by Nina Mata.
     p. cm. -- (Readers' theater: how to put on a production)
  ISBN 978-1-61641-990-5
1. Snow White (Tale)--Adaptations--Juvenile drama. 2. Fairy tales--Adaptations--Juvenile drama. 3. Theater--Production and direction--Juvenile literature. 4. Readers' theater--Juvenile literature. I. Mata, Nina, 1981- illustrator. II. Title.
  PS3623.A4436S58 2013
  812'.6--dc23
                                                    2013006053

Table of Contents

School Plays

Do you like to act, create props, make weird sound effects, or paint scenery? You should put on a production. Plays are lots of fun! And a play is a great way for kids to work together as a team.

Readers' theater can be done very simply. You just read your lines. You don't have to memorize them! Adapted readers' theater looks more like a regular play. The performers wear makeup and costumes. The stage has scenery and props. The cast moves around to show the action. But, performers still read their scripts.

You will need a space large enough to put on your production. An auditorium with a stage is ideal. A classroom will work, too. Now, choose a date and get permission to use the space.

Finally, make flyers or posters to advertise your play. Place them around your school and community. Don't forget to tell your friends and family!

Cast & Crew

There are many people needed to put on a production. First, decide who will play each part. Each person in the cast will need a script. All the performers should practice their lines.

Snow White and the Seven Dorks has a lot of speaking parts.

Announcer - Introduces the play and announces each scene

Narrator - The storyteller

Snow White - A beautiful, young princess

King - Snow White's father

Queen Leticia - An evil witch

Mirror - A magical mirror that Queen Leticia uses

The Dorks - Six brothers who are computer geeks - Grumpy, Lumpy, Chumpy, Frumpy, Dumpy, Jumpy

Howard - the Dorks' adopted brother

Next, a crew is needed. The show can't go on without these important people! Some jobs can be combined for a small show. Every show needs a director. This person organizes everything and everyone in the show.

The director works with the production crew. This includes the costume designers, who borrow or make all the costumes. Stage managers make sure things run smoothly.

Your production can also have a stage crew. This includes lighting designers to run spotlights and other lighting. Set designers plan and make scenery. The special effects crew takes care of sound and other unusual effects.

Sets & Props

At a readers' theater production, the performers sit on stools at the front of the room. But, an adapted readers' theater production or full play will require some sets and props.

Sets include a background for each scene of the play. Props are things you'll need during the play. You'll also need tickets that list important information. Be sure to include the title of the play and where it will take place. List the date and the time of your performance. Print the price of the ticket if you are charging a fee to attend.

Your production can also have a playbill. It is a printed program. The front of a playbill has the title, date, and time of the play. Playbills list all of the cast and production team inside.

Snow White and the Seven Dorks could have the following sets and props:

Scene Sets - A castle made of cardboard at center stage and a forest of cardboard or fake trees. The last scene takes place at the Dorks' house. It should have several desks and computers. See if your school has old monitors and keyboards that you could use. Make seven beds by putting blankets and pillows on the floor. The Dorks need a table with seven chairs where they eat breakfast.

Props - For the Magic Mirror, you will need a large picture frame without glass in it. You could also make one out of cardboard. You will need a basket of red apples for Queen Leticia. Put plastic or paper plates on the Dorks' kitchen table. Make a giant pair of red lips from poster board or construction paper for Howard. Glue them to a wooden paint stick.

Makeup & Costumes

The stage and props aren't the only things people will be looking at in your play. The makeup artist has a big job. Stage makeup needs to be brighter than regular makeup. Even boys wear stage makeup!

Costume designers set the scene just as much as set designers. They borrow costumes or adapt old clothing for each character. Ask adults if you need help finding or sewing costumes.

Snow White and the Seven Dorks performers will need these costumes:

Announcer - Designer's choice

Narrator - A shirt and pants with a cloak

Snow White - A long dress, a crown, and a cloak for the forest

King - A crown and a fancy shirt

Queen Leticia - A long dress, a crown, and a cloak for her disguise

Mirror - Black pants and a black top. The person playing the Mirror holds the picture frame so his face shows through the opening

The Dorks - Grumpy, Lumpy, Chumpy, Frumpy, Dumpy, and Jumpy - Matching T-shirts, funny hats, or glasses. Add poster board name tags on strings for the Dorks to wear around their necks

Howard - Match the dorks and add a hat or a wig for him to remove in the last act

Stage Directions

When all of your sets, props, and costumes are ready, it is important to rehearse. Choose a time that everyone can attend. Try to have at least five or six rehearsals before your show.

You should practice together as a team even if you will be reading your scripts for readers' theater. A play should sound like a conversation. Try to avoid pauses when no one is speaking. You can do this by adding sound effects.

Some theater terms may seem strange. The *wings* are the sides of the stage that the audience can't see. The *house* is where the audience sits. The *curtains* refers to the main curtain at the front of the stage.

When reading your script, the stage directions are in parentheses. They are given from the performer's point of view. You will be facing the audience when you are performing. Left will be on your left and right will be on your right. When rehearsing, perform the stage directions and the lines to get used to moving around the stage.

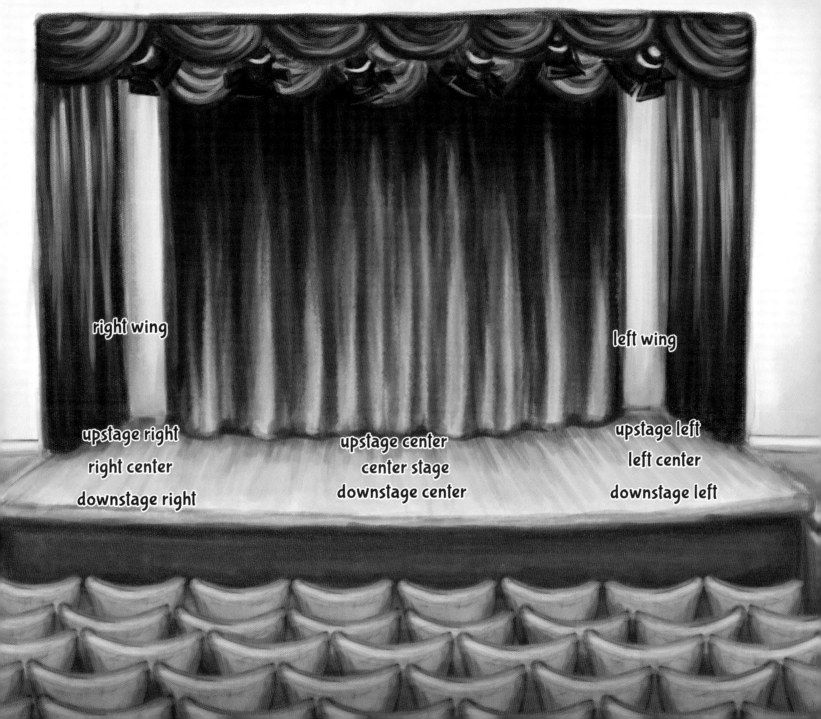

right wing

left wing

upstage right

right center

downstage right

upstage center

center stage

downstage center

upstage left

left center

downstage left

Script: *Snow White* and the *Seven Dorks*

(Opening of the Curtain: Snow White sits alone reading on a chair at center stage. The narrator sits on a stool at stage right removed from the action.)

Announcer: Snow White and the Seven Dorks—Scene 1—The Castle

Narrator: *(Points at Snow White)* Once upon a time, a beautiful princess named Snow White lived with her father, the king. They lived in an awesome castle on the edge of a lake. Her mother, the queen, had passed away some years before. One day, the king went away on a long trip. When he returned he brought back a new wife.

King: *(King enters with Queen Leticia)* Snow White, this is my new wife, Queen Leticia. She will be your stepmother.

Snow White: *(Stands and bows)* Welcome to our castle!

Queen Leticia: *(Coldly)* Thank you, Snow White.

Snow White: I will ask the cook to prepare a special dinner in your honor! Any woman my father loves must be a very good woman.

(Snow White and the king exit.)

Narrator: But Snow White was wrong. Queen Leticia was really a beautiful witch, who had charmed the king into marrying her. *(The Magic Mirror enters.)* On Queen Leticia's first day, she set up her magic mirror. She asked it the question she asked it every morning.

Queen Leticia: *(Faces mirror)* Mirror, Mirror, look at me. Am I the loveliest that you see?

Mirror: Your beauty was beyond compare. But now another is more fair.

Queen Leticia: *(Angrily)* What? I don't believe you! How could anyone be more beautiful than me?

Mirror: Snow White is pure and good and true. She's far more beautiful than you.

Queen Leticia: *(Stamping her foot)* No one more beautiful than me will be allowed to live in this kingdom! I will make Snow White's life miserable! Then maybe she will leave and I will have the king to myself. *(Queen exits)*

Scene change: Stage crew closes curtain and replaces the castle with a forest. Scene two is performed in front of the closed curtain.

Announcer: Scene 2—Inside the Castle

(Snow White is on her knees scrubbing the floor.)

Narrator: And so, Queen Leticia made Snow White's life miserable. She gave away all of her beautiful clothes and made the princess dress in rags.

Snow White: I look like a beggar in these clothes. Now, I eat in the kitchen and work like a servant.

Narrator: And worst of all, Queen Leticia banished Snow White's boyfriend, Prince Rupert, from the kingdom.

Snow White: *(Crying)* My father doesn't even notice how she treats me. I have no one left who I can trust. Tomorrow, I will run away and find Prince Rupert! *(Snow White exits)*

Scene change: The curtain opens to show the forest.

Announcer: Scene 3—The Forest

Narrator: The next night, Snow White waited until the castle was dark and quiet. She packed a few things and set off into the forest.

Snow White: *(Snow White enters)* I've never been this far from the castle before. I'm so scared!

Narrator: Now, it was winter and the night was very cold. Soon, small snowflakes drifted down. Snow White was hopelessly lost.

(Stage crew can throw small bits of white paper or fake snowflakes on the stage around Snow White.)

Snow White: I am so cold. I don't know what to do. *(Walks slowly across the stage)*

Narrator: As she wandered, she saw a light through the trees. As she came closer, she saw it was a little cottage with satellite dishes on the roof. Snow White knocked at the door.

Snow White: *(Pretends to knock at an imaginary door. Sound crew makes knocking noise.)* Oh, I hope a kind person will let me come in!

Scene change: The curtain closes for set up of the Dorks' house. Scene opens with all the dorks except Grumpy sleeping on the floor with their pillows and blankets.

Announcer: Scene 4—The Dorks' House

Grumpy: Who's there? Do you realize how late it is?

Snow White: It's Snow White. Can I come in, please?

Grumpy: Just a minute, I'm logging off.

Narrator: When the door opened, Snow White saw a strange little man. The room was filled with computers. Wires ran all over the floor. She stepped inside.

Grumpy: Hi, I'm Grumpy. You've reached the Dork Squad. Are you having trouble with your computer?

Snow White: I don't have a computer.

Grumpy: Then why are you here? All we do is fix computers.

Snow White: I'm lost. I'm looking for somewhere to spend the night.

Grumpy: Well, the house is kind of full already. I live here with my six brothers: Lumpy, Frumpy, Chumpy, Dumpy, Jumpy, and Howard.

Snow White: Could I stay just for tonight? It's snowing outside.

Grumpy: Well, I suppose so. I'll be up all night. I'm taking the late shift. My bed's right over there. I'll just get back to my computers.

Snow White: You're very kind.

Narrator: Snow White spent the night at the Dork Squad's house. In the morning, she got up very early and fixed a nice breakfast. The dorks wakened to the smell of bread baking, bacon frying, and eggs cooking. They were surprised to see Snow White in their kitchen.

(Snow White walks in from stage right and puts plates out on the table. The Dorks sit up and stretch and yawn.)

Lumpy: Something smells really good! *(He stands up and sees Snow White.)* Oh, who are you?

Grumpy: This is Snow White. She was lost in the forest last night.

Lumpy: Hi, Snow White! Where do you live? I'd be glad to help you find your way home.

Snow White: I don't want to go home.

All Dorks: Why not?

(The Dorks sit down at the table while the narrator is talking.)

Narrator: So, Snow White told the seven dorks all about her new stepmother and how she didn't want to live at the castle anymore.

Chumpy: Why don't you just live with us, Snow White? This food is fantastic!

Frumpy: We could use someone to take care of us. We spend all our time fixing computers. It would be nice to have a hot meal every once in a while.

Dumpy: I'll even give you my bed. We all sleep on the floor anyway. Why don't you stay?

Snow White: Well, all right, I will stay here. Thank you very much!

(All Dorks exit except Grumpy, who sits down at one of the computers. Snow White clears the table.)

Narrator: So every day, Snow White cooked and baked and kept the little house tidy for her new friends. At night, the Dorks taught her all about computers and the Internet. All except Howard, who just looked very sad and never said anything at all. Finally, Snow White asked Grumpy about Howard.

Snow White: What's the matter with Howard?

Grumpy: I don't know. We think he is under a spell. He hasn't talked since he came here.

Snow White: But I thought he was one of your brothers.

Grumpy: We found him wandering in the forest. We adopted him.

Snow White: You adopted me, too. You Dorks are just the best! *(Snow White gives Grumpy a hug.)*

(Grumpy exits. Snow White sits down to read a book.)

Narrator: One day, all seven dorks went to a technology conference. They left Snow White alone for three days. They warned her about not opening the door to strangers and locking the house at night. Snow White didn't have to cook or bake very much since the Dorks were away, so she decided to surf the Internet.

Snow White: Oh! I discovered this great Web site. Maybe if I make my own page, Prince Rupert will see it and try to contact me.

Narrator: Snow White put the Dorks' address and phone number on her new page. She spent all afternoon and evening on the computer hoping to receive some information from Prince Rupert. Late the next afternoon, there was a knock at the door.

Snow White: Oh, maybe that is Prince Rupert! Who's there?

Queen Leticia: *(Disguising her voice)* Just an old woman selling winter apples, my dear. Would you like some?

Snow White: I would love some apples! I'd like to bake a pie for the seven Dorks. They have been so kind to me.

Narrator: Snow White didn't realize that the old woman was really her stepmother. Queen Leticia had seen Snow White's page. She was angry that Snow White still lived in the kingdom and she had come to give her a poisoned apple. *(Snow White opens the door.)*

Queen Leticia: *(Holds out an apple.)* Here, my dear. Just taste one of these lovely apples.

Snow White: They are beautiful and red. They look very tasty!

Narrator: Snow White took a bite of the apple and immediately fell to the floor in a deep sleep. (*Snow White collapses on the floor.*)

(*Queen walks off the stage and exits.*)

Narrator: It was early the next morning before the seven little men returned. (*Dorks enter and stand around Snow White.*) They found Snow White lying as still as death on the floor with the poisoned apple beside her.

Grumpy: Oh no, I think she ate a poisoned apple!

Chumpy: I'll bet Queen Leticia was here! What should we do?

Lumpy: What's the cure for poisoned apples?

Dumpy: Check the Internet!

Narrator: So Chumpy looked online.

Chumpy: It says she needs a kiss from her true love.

Jumpy: And who would that be?

Narrator: Just then Howard stepped forward. *(Howard holds up the giant lips on the paint stick and touches Snow White's mouth with them.)* He leaned over and kissed Snow White right on the lips. The Dorks were amazed!

Frumpy: Howard!

Lumpy: Wow! That was some kiss!

Jumpy: I didn't even know you liked her!

Grumpy: Look, Snow White's waking up! Maybe she'll be okay!

Narrator: Just as Snow White was beginning to rub her eyes and sit up, Howard began to look a little different. *(Howard takes off his wig or hat.)* He was smiling and his eyes twinkled. He looked just like Snow White's boyfriend, Prince Rupert. Snow White was delighted!

Snow White: Prince Rupert, I found you, at last!

Grumpy: I'm confused. You mean Howard was Prince Rupert all along?

Howard: Snow White's stepmother put a spell on me. She changed the way I looked and I couldn't talk! I could never tell anyone what had happened to me.

Chumpy: Wow! Snow White's stepmother was a meanie!

Grumpy: I don't understand how Queen Leticia found you, Snow White. We tried so hard to protect you.

Snow White: It's all my fault. I made a Web page to try to find Prince Rupert.

Lumpy: Didn't we tell you that anyone can read that stuff?

Frumpy: You have to be very careful what you post online!

Snow White: I know. I'm sorry. But now I don't need it anymore! I have Prince Rupert back.

Lumpy: I read online that the queen was deported for identity theft. You can go back to the castle and live with your father and Prince Rupert!

Snow White: But, I will miss you. I have an idea! Why don't you come to live at the castle? I think my father needs the Dork Squad to bring his kingdom into the twenty-first century! *(Everyone exits except the narrator.)*

Narrator: And so Snow White went home to live with her father, who had missed her very much. In a few years, she married Prince Rupert. The Dork Squad set up shop in the east tower with a cutting-edge security system. It had a special Queen Leticia detector to keep everyone safe. And they all lived happily ever after!

The End

Adapting Readers' Theater Scripts

Readers' theater can be done very simply. You just read your lines. You don't have to memorize them! Performers sit on chairs or stools. They read their parts without moving around.

Adapted Readers' Theater

This looks more like a regular play. The performers wear makeup and costumes. The stage has scenery and props. The cast moves around to show the action. Performers can still read their scripts.

Hold a Puppet Show

Some schools and libraries have puppet collections. Students make the puppets be the actors. Performers can read their scripts.

Teacher's Guides

Readers' Theater Teacher's Guides are available online. Each guide includes reading levels for each character and additional production tips for each play. Visit Teacher's Guides at **www.abdopublishing.com** to get yours today!